M000002647

Dancing with Demons

GINGER LEIGH DAVIES

authorHOUSE

AuthorHouse™
1663 Liberty Drive
Bloomington, IN 47403
www.authorhouse.com
Phone: 833-262-8899

© 2020 Ginger Leigh Davies. All rights reserved.

No part of this book may be reproduced, stored in a retrieval system, or transmitted by any means without the written permission of the author.

Published by AuthorHouse 09/29/2020

ISBN: 978-1-7283-7036-1 (sc)
ISBN: 978-1-7283-7034-7 (e)

Library of Congress Control Number: 2020915286

Print information available on the last page.

This book is printed on acid-free paper.

Because of the dynamic nature of the Internet, any web addresses or links contained in this book may have changed since publication and may no longer be valid. The views expressed in this work are solely those of the author and do not necessarily reflect the views of the publisher, and the publisher hereby disclaims any responsibility for them.

About the Author

Raised a nomad of sorts, Ginger spent many hours lost in books to hide emotions. Over time the catharsis evolved into writing to work through emotional issues. She shares with readers a view inside the chrysalis as she faces inner demons in a tumultuous tango wrought with trials and tribulations in search of truth—a mercurial dance ending triumphantly on a note of confident self-acceptance. Come soar in the colorful world of vibrant feelings as she spreads her wings and learns to fly.

Dancing Leaves

As I watch leaves joust the wind,
Whirling and twirling they riposte that blade;
Like life, waltz 'twixt light and shade.
Why must the dance always end the same?
Alone, in the dark afraid.

Life Song

Sing and dance to life's tune—
Such sweet music ends too soon.
Waste no wishes on the stars or moon.
Set Joy free of Fear's cocoon.

The soul writes your life's song,
Beating a rhythm lilting and strong.
Softly the heart sings for what it longs;
Judge not Serendipity so wrong.

Each dreary day and every lonely night,
Angels wept as our melancholy songs took flight.
Those beatific tears led us here, weary knight.
Come and rest your spirit until comes the night;
Our hearts sing again with audacious delight.

Dockside Dismay

At day's end as sun sets again,
bereft souls are left to ponder: when
Will the spirits hear and call the wind
To hasten a loved one's journey's end?

But the dark currents are beset
with pirates that loot the hearts of men,
Leaving many lonely maidens
On vacant shores mourning them.

Demonic Love

Disarming smile and inviting eyes,
With calloused hands that hypnotize,
Draw forth passions that paralyze.
Whispers drift over fevered flesh as I yield,
abandoned by distant daylight's shield.

Unconfined wild ecstasy buffeting
Sets to flight wings now fluttering,
Searing denied need in a fiery bath,
Inviting me to journey down a dark path.

Entranced, timid, and demanding,
I press against you, heedless of warning,
Flooding my body with heated wanting
Lighting the fuse of my need abruptly,
Burning fires of passions erupting.

I woke throbbing and glowing,
My sleepy release juices flowing.
His image blocking light from my window sill,
Savage kisses linger on lips that hunger still.

Languidly I yield the wonder,
Dreaded daylight casts it asunder,
Stealing joy as a pirate plunders.

My hunger and need bid the philistine farewell,
Driving this captivated soul to a sultry hell.
I rush to intoxicating, dark, demanding desires,
To the arms of a demon lover and his demonic fire.

Only Yours

Reach for me when you are weary;
Let my faith defeat doubts dreary;
Watch my fiery heart melt fear's fury.

You could demand, of course;
Alas, you've no need for force—
I am already completely yours.

I offer you a simple gift,
Only asking this:
Warm me with your sunlit smiles
As I submit to your dominant wiles.

Maestro's Orchestration

He listens to unvoiced needs and desires unknown,
Conducting my mind and body in concert with his own,

Setting a tempo to scale the heights of sensuality,
Eliciting nuanced phrasing audaciously,

Directing each note over my skin and through my soul—
My submission's a symphony under his control.

Early Morning

In darkness I hear you whisper,
Lost in the subtle caress.
Warm breath dances over flesh,
each wave fueling wanton distress.

On the morrow as the sun wakes,
a gentle rain revives the erotic ache.

Each warm drop's descent over my skin,
Waking hungered passions within,
Longing to feel your demonic fire again

I turn to you with sleepy, sultry smile,
Nakedness pressed against you to beguile.

Your kiss still heady with my taste
Releases molten memories driving desire's haste.

Pulling away I move deftly
to begin trailing kisses down intently,
Scorching your soul with anticipation:
Your torture ends at my destination.

My prize your ragged gasp,
I take you in my gentle clasp,
Lips parted to let you feel warm wetness
while my sensual assault leaves you breathless.

The Weaver

Shimmering tapestry of feigned indifference,
woven warp and weft of willowy yarn,
spun on the wheel of pain with fallen tears,
each a lesson learned from storms long passed.

Gimmering shroud guards a dark well,
the abyss of unspoken desires, dark and dangerous.
Delicate defense consumed in the conflagration,
ignited by the piercing fiery demon's gaze,
surrendered to the heat of illicit longing.

Amidst the scattered embers and ash
shivers a hungered spirit in tattered remnants,
child of hope and dreams
long ago abandoned, denied, all but forgotten.

Resuscitated by the warm and caressing flames,
a casualty of the demonic assault,
sad creature, betrayer of needs and desires,
Longs for comfort hidden within.

As cooling breezes see away passions spent,
in blow shadows of remembered fears,
unbidden,
unwanted,
unrelenting.

Dismissing the brief sunlight of loving bliss,
conjuring spectres of uncertainty and self-doubt.

Ominous rumbling tremors reverberate
within that lost soul's breast bereft.
Thunder echoes loudly in the mind;
as spinning wheel springs to life,
the first raindrop falls.

Fading Embers

As the flames of a dream die,
only these sad tendrils remain,
smoke curling up from the cinders.

Silent insidious reminders of emptiness
the space once full of wonder and dreams.

Entrusted to strong, calloused, yet once gentle hands,
only burnt shards remain of that fragile gift.

Worry not, for fading embers portend their own death.
Soon too shall I follow.

Departing Demon

The setting sun casts its long shadow
from the ivory tower where we lived.

Cloaking memories that once glowed,
leaving only coldness deep within.

Enchantments fade as our days depart,
and frost claims this broken heart.

Go now, darling demon, lover, friend,
as too your soul must descend.

Return to the darkness cheerfully;
I bid you farewell tearfully.

Acceptance

Felled by forgotten fears
In the river of unbidden tears,
Abandoned the fervent belief
Prayers could bring relief.

Pain and sorrow left to solder,
Hope's flame grows colder.
Anguished acceptance and more
Seeks warmth on distant shores.

Honesty and trust were tokens,
But betrayal leaves me broken.
Surging swells scattered shards about,
Embraced darkly by spectres of self-doubt.

Knowing tearful protests come too late;
With head bowed, accept this lonely fate.

Dream Darkly

Night dreams yield to waking mind.
Sparkling dew on landscape shines,
Reminding all to taste life's sweet wine.

The morning star burns my liquid shield.
Without ephemeral defense I yield,
No champion to Hope on Love's battlefield.

Shattered fragments of fragile gift
Lay scattered wide and set adrift.

Remnants of baubles naively given now render
A poignant piercing portrait of a heart so tender.

Each pain endured and long-forgotten fears
Reflect and refract light to blind with unbidden tears.

Moisture evaporates as pain lingers on,
Sad memories like the sun's warmth now gone.

Soft strains of darkness a siren's song
Promising comfort to those who still long,

Beguiled dreamers, unable to turn away,
Mourn not loss of day.

One questions through sorrow,
Must I wake on the morrow?

Dark Rivers

In the solitude of darkness,
Dreamers mourn lost happiness.
Abandoned on a path now cold,
Inviting melancholia's hold.

Emotional rivers drown rational thought,
Silencing dreamers with watery garrote,
Liquid graves for the broken and distraught.

Worry not, gentle folk; afore long,
Greet again the bastion strong.
A masque of living devoid of tears,
Emotions hidden to ease your fears.

Receding waters leave only frigid intellectuality.
Sad home to shattered dreams and whimsicality.
Sanctuary to the dreamer's battered emotionality.

Day's End

Watching the sun set tonight,
pondering how to set aright
all the tomorrows gone,
abandoned, we journey on.

Dawn again yet finds
Love so strong and kind.
A silent centurion through the dark—
night's abyss extinguishes not his spark,
Lighting each new morning sky
without ever asking why.

A Final Masterpiece

Indifference and detachment surround her.
Blades slashing with determination,
Clearing a path for the quiet observer,
Unburdened by emotional indignation.

Studying lost vibrancy with curious intent.
The vivid trail of each drop's decent,
To the vibrant crimson painting 'neath now cold hand.
Artist embraced in darkness his masterpiece so grand.
Illicit the soft query
Whispered almost inaudibly:

Why does blood F
A
L
L
soundlessly?

Director's Advice

The piper must always be paid.
Though Serendipity be not stayed,
Continue, dear thespian, to ply thy trade.

Shadow not life's plot with rage.
Pen each new act on a fresh page.
Live each moment free of that cage—

Lest you find, as footlights fade,
Your revolt gone the way of Jack Cade's.

Failing Fate

In darkness when silence's embrace pulls you near,
And capricious fates thieve all once held dear,
An inner voice still drives us ever onward without fear.
Though wounded, the human spirit's unrivaled resiliency
Allows not fleeting pain to halt its transcendency.

Sweet Sunshine

Goodbye, sweet sunshine;
On the horizon you decline.

While storm clouds gather and align,
Shadows cast about only find
A soul broken and resigned.

I shall dance my life,
Consort only to demons confined,
Snarling with rage inside my mind.

Goodbye, sweet sunshine;
Be free, beautiful dream of mine.

The Hungered Heart

A future full and serene
Felled by a slash so keen.
Leaving only searing anguish
Yearning to be extinguished.

As I lay 'neath the willow weeping,
There came a dark knight creeping.
He stilled my hand without force,
Whispering with chilled remorse;

"Time has not come to take this course.
Your pain, sweet child, is slight,
compared to that eternal night."

My hand, now stayed by loss of will,
holds a heart that hungers still.

Dreams of Flying

In darkness slips a fraction of time,
A whole life lived in dreams sublime.

Remember in the darkest night
When the heart longs to take flight,
Before a soul can fly,
It need only courage to spread its wings and try.

Rough Diamonds

Everyone has a diamond inside.
Life is the polish that makes it shine.
Flickering and refracted rhymes,
Are joyful moments danced through time.

Mindful Melody

Shimmering dew on new green grass,
a thousand notes that glisten,
Untouchable beauties fleeting and fragile,
So too this forgotten melody: Listen!

Soft and rich with piercing poignancy,
a languid rhythm full
with memories and musings.

A waltz of endless spinning,
crescendos woven through decrescendos.

Comes now a sprightly refrain,
the delicate consort with cheerful cadence—

Entwining exuberant **FORTISSIMO**,
and twirling timid *pianissimo*.

The lilting strains for a lifetime of dance
play forever in the mind.

Empty Space

In the emptiness I see you,
While reading and wandering through.
Did you enjoy the breathtaking view?
In the space between words I called for you.
An emotional kaleidoscope paints the world I run to.
Once you've read the lyrics,
Won't you come sing with me too?

CPSIA information can be obtained
at www.ICGtesting.com
Printed in the USA
JSHW030046101020
8656JS00001B/19